W9-DGS-833

Plants

Roots

Patricia Whitehouse

Heinemann Library
Chicago, Illinois

What Are Roots?

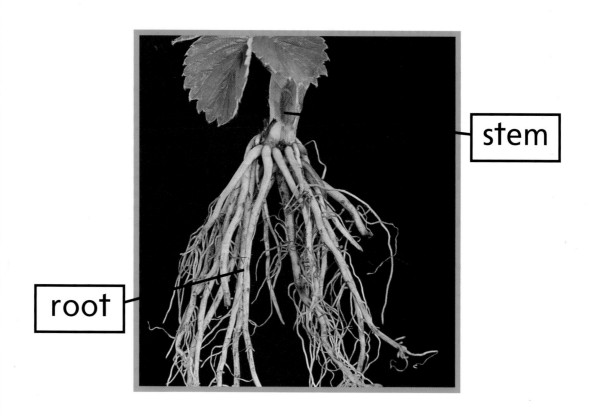

stem

root

Roots are parts of plants that are under the **stem.**

Most roots are underground.

Some roots are in water.

Some roots are in air.

Why Do Plants Have Roots?

root hairs

Roots store food for plants.

The **root hairs** soak up the water plants need.

Roots hold plants in place so they don't tip over.

Where Do Roots Come From?

seed

root

Roots come from seeds.

Roots are the first plant part that comes out of a seed.

leaf

stem

root

Some plants can grow roots from their **stems**.

Other plants can grow roots from their leaves.

How Big Are Roots?

Roots come in many sizes.

Grass roots are short and thin.

Some roots are long.

Big, long roots like carrots are called **taproots.**

How Many Roots Can Plants Have?

radish

corn

Some plants have one root.

Some plants have more.

Some plants may have hundreds of roots.

What Shapes Are Roots?

Some roots are round.

Some roots look like hair.

The root of this ginger plant is shaped like a person!

What Colors Are Roots?

Roots can be many colors.

Some roots are red.

Sweet potatoes are orange.

How Do People Use Roots?

People use roots for food.

When you eat carrots, you are eating roots.

Some people eat roots raw.

Some eat baked or fried roots.

How Do Animals Use Roots?

Animals use roots for food, too.

Animals also use roots for hiding.

They use roots to make their homes.

Quiz

Can you remember what these root parts are called?

Look for the answers on page 24.

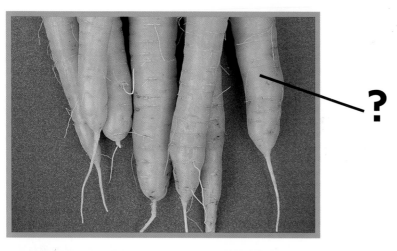

?

?

Picture Glossary

 **root hairs**
page 6

 **stem**
pages 4, 9

 **taproot**
page 11

Note to Parents and Teachers

Reading for information is an important part of a child's literacy development. Learning begins with a question about something. Help children think of themselves as investigators and researchers by encouraging their questions about the world around them. Each chapter in this book begins with a question. Read the question together. Look at the pictures. Talk about what you think the answer might be. Then read the text to find out if your predictions were correct. Think of other questions you could ask about the topic, and discuss where you might find the answers. Assist children in using the picture glossary and the index to practice new vocabulary and research skills.

Index

Answers to quiz on page 22

taproot

root hairs